PROUDLY DESIGNED ON THE UPPER WEST SIDE
(OF KANSAS CITY).

A MILLION* THINGS TO DO BEFORE YOU DIE OR JUST GET OLD & BORING.

A PROMPTED JOURNAL

DISCLAIMER

X X X

WE MADE THIS JOURNAL TO TRY TO
INSPIRE A BIT OF FUN IN THIS WORLD,
BECAUSE HONESTLY—IT NEEDS IT.

THINK OF THIS AS OUR LITTLE WAY OF
GETTING PEOPLE TO BREAK OUT OF THEIR
DAILY ROUTINES AND STOP TAKING
EVERYTHING (INCLUDING THEMSELVES)
SO SERIOUSLY. OUR DAYS ARE NUMBERED
(LITERALLY) SO LET'S ALL MAKE THE
MOST OF IT—AND ACTUALLY ENJOY LIFE.

THAT SAID, DON'T TAKE THIS THING TOO
LITERALLY. WHILE EVERYTHING WE
PUT IN HERE WOULD PROBABLY BE REALLY
FUN TO DO—SOME OF IT MIGHT NOT BE
EXACTLY 'LEGAL' OR WHAT THEY CALL
'SOCIALLY ACCEPTABLE BEHAVIOR'.

SO USE THIS BOOK AS INSPIRATION,
NOT AS INSTRUCTIONS. A PREREQUISITE
HERE IS COMMON SENSE (AND A SENSE
OF HUMOR). DON'T DO ANYTHING THAT'S
ILLEGAL, OR THAT WOULD EMBARRASS
AND/OR HURT OTHERS...AND WE'RE NOT
RESPONSIBLE IF YOU DO.

ANYWAY, HAVE FUN...AND KEEP GOING
WHERE WE LEFT OFF. IN FACT, WE GAVE
YOU SOME SPACE TO ADD YOUR OWN 'MUST
DOS' IN THE BACK OF THE BOOK. WE'D
LOVE TO SEE WHAT YOU COME UP WITH.

@ BRASSMONKEYGOODS

THIS JOURNAL IS DEDICATED
TO ALL OF THE TALENTED PEOPLE
THAT HAVE INSPIRED US OVER
THE YEARS — BUT WHO ARE SADLY NO
LONGER WITH US. SO MITCH, HARRIS,
NORM, AND COUNTLESS OTHERS...

X X X

THANKS FOR EVERYTHING.

HOW TO USE THIS JOURNAL

A TUTORIAL

THE GOAL OF THIS BOOK IS SIMPLE: TO INSPIRE A LITTLE BIT OF FUN IN THE WORLD. THAT'S IT, AND NOTHING MORE. WE HAVE NO AGENDA. NO BROADER MESSAGE TO SELL. WE JUST WANT PEOPLE TO SMILE AND ENJOY BEING ALIVE...NO MATTER HOW STUPID LIFE CAN BE SOMETIMES.

SPOILER ALERT: REALLY STUPID.

WE KNOW, THERE ARE THOUSANDS OF 'THINGS TO DO BEFORE YOU DIE' LISTS ALREADY OUT THERE. TRUST US, WE'VE BEEN READING THEM FOR YEARS. SO WHY ANOTHER ONE? WELL, WE COULD JUST NEVER UNDERSTAND WHY THEY HAD TO BE SO BORING. HOW CAN LISTS ABOUT DOING CRAZY THINGS BEFORE YOU DIE ALL BE SO SERIOUS?

SO THAT'S WHERE THIS JOURNAL COMES IN.

WE'VE DONE OUR BEST TO PACK THIS ONE FULL OF THE KIND OF THINGS THAT WE'VE ALWAYS WISHED THAT WE COULD DO. A FEW ARE SWEET, A LOT ARE WEIRD, AND SOME MIGHT EVEN BE DAMN NEAR IMPOSSIBLE TO PULL OFF. THAT'S BECAUSE THIS BOOK IS ABOUT THE SPIRIT OF THE IDEA, NOT THE ACTUAL THING THAT'S WRITTEN DOWN.

SO GO THROUGH THE BOOK, AND JUST HAVE FUN. COMPLETE AS MANY OF THEM AS YOU CAN. WE'VE EVEN INCLUDED SPACE FOR YOU TO GIVE YOUR REVIEW OF THE EXPERIENCE. AS YOU DO THEM THOUGH, PLEASE SHARE PICTURES, VIDEOS, AND ANY STORIES WITH YOUR FRIENDS (AND US @ BRASSMONKEYGOODS). WE'D LOVE TO DO OUR PART TO HELP THE INTERNET FEEL LESS LIKE THE WORLD IS ENDING AND EVERYTHING IS TERRIBLE.

REMEMBER THAT DISCLAIMER? WELL, IT'S BACK AGAIN: A PREREQUISITE HERE IS COMMON SENSE (AND A SENSE OF HUMOR). DON'T DO ANYTHING ILLEGAL, OR ANYTHING THAT WOULD EMBARRASS OR HURT OTHERS...AND WE'RE NOT RESPONSIBLE IF YOU DO. WE'RE HERE TO INSPIRE FUN, NOT LAWSUITS.

GET FORCIBLY REMOVED FROM
AN ALL YOU CAN EAT BUFFET FOR
EATING TOO MUCH.

WHAT'S YOUR REVIEW?

RUN AND DIVE TOWARDS THE PINS
AT A BOWLING ALLEY. ALSO, GET KICKED
OUT OF A BOWLING ALLEY.

WHAT'S YOUR REVIEW?

WALK AROUND GEORGIA WITH A
FIDDLE, ASKING EVERYONE IF THEY'VE
SEEN THE DEVIL.

WHAT'S YOUR REVIEW?

GO TO TACO BELL AND ORDER
ONE OF EVERYTHING ON THE MENU.
FOR DINE-IN.

WHAT'S YOUR REVIEW?

OBJECT AT THE END OF SOMEONE'S
WEDDING. WHEN THEY ASK FOR THE REASON,
JUST YELL 'TOO ADORABLE' AND RUN.

WHAT'S YOUR REVIEW?

GO TO A FANCY FRENCH RESTAURANT & DRAW A PICTURE OF YOUR ORDER FOR YOUR WAITER INSTEAD OF HORRIBLY MISPRONOUNCING IT.

DON'T HAVE A CANVAS HANDY? USE THIS:

SIGN YOUR MASTERPIECE

WRITE DOWN ALL OF YOUR FAVORITE MEMORIES AND GET IT SELF-PUBLISHED AS A BOOK FOR YOUR COFFEE TABLE.

MAKE A SNOWMAN WITH FRESHLY FALLEN SNOW — BUT DON'T USE THE CARROT FOR HIS NOSE.

. . . .

. . . .

. . . .

. . . .

. . . .

. . . .

WHAT'S YOUR REVIEW?

HANG A MAP ON YOUR WALL AND THROW A DART AT IT. DRIVE TO WHERE EVER IT LANDS, RIGHT AFTER YOU PATCH THAT HOLE.

. . . .

. . . .

. . . .

. . . .

. . . .

. . . .

WHAT'S YOUR REVIEW?

WATCH THE SUN SET AND RISE AGAIN IN THE SAME NIGHT—UNLESS YOU ALREADY HAVE TO WORK NIGHTS.

— WHAT'S YOUR REVIEW? —

TAKE A LOAF OF STALE BREAD TO THE PARK, RIP IT UP IN LITTLE PIECES, AND FEED ALL OF THE HUMANS WALKING AROUND.

— WHAT'S YOUR REVIEW? —

ORDER AN EXTRA LARGE PIZZA AND EAT THE WHOLE THING YOURSELF. AGAIN. BUT THIS TIME IT'S FOR A REASON.

— WHAT'S YOUR REVIEW? —

RUN A FULL MARATHON.
OR WALK A FULL MARATHON.
OKAY, WATCH A MOVIE MARATHON.

WHAT'S YOUR REVIEW?

EXHIBIT A

GET A CELEBRITY TO GIVE YOU THE FINGER GUNS — WE'RE TALKING AT LEAST A C-LISTER. NOW DRAW WHAT THEY LOOKED LIKE.

DON'T HAVE A CANVAS HANDY? USE THIS:

SIGN YOUR MASTERPIECE

DO A DONUT IN THE PARKING LOT OF A DONUT SHOP.

WHAT'S YOUR REVIEW?

EAT A DONUT IN THE PARKING LOT OF A 24 HOUR FITNESS.

WHAT'S YOUR REVIEW?

RAKE ALL OF THE LEAVES FROM YOUR NEIGHBORHOOD INTO ONE ENORMOUS PILE AND JUMP INTO THEM.

WHAT'S YOUR REVIEW?

EXHIBIT A

**BUY A JAR OF MARMITE AND
FINALLY FIGURE OUT WHAT THE HELL
IT TASTES LIKE.**

. . . .

. . . .

——————— WHAT'S YOUR REVIEW? ———————

**VISIT ALL 63 NATIONAL PARKS IN THE
U.S. AND FORCE A PARK RANGER TO TAKE
A PHOTO WITH YOU.**

. . . .

. . . .

——————— WHAT'S YOUR REVIEW? ———————

**FIND A VACANT LOT & PLANT A TREE FOR EACH
YEAR THAT YOU'VE BEEN ALIVE.* MAKE A
PLAQUE & NAME THE FOREST AFTER YOURSELF.**

*WITH PERMISSION OF COURSE. HAPPY NOW, LAWYERS?

. . . .

. . . .

——————— WHAT'S YOUR REVIEW? ———————

TAKE A SWIM IN EACH ONE OF
THE GREAT LAKES. GO AHEAD AND PEE A
LITTLE WHILE YOU'RE IN THERE.

WHAT'S YOUR REVIEW?

DRINK A GIANT BOOT FULL OF BEER.
SPECIFICALLY, A GLASS THAT'S SHAPED LIKE A
BOOT. ACTUAL SHOES AREN'T RECOMMENDED.

WHAT'S YOUR REVIEW?

GO TO THE BEACH AND YELL 'SHARK!...WEEK IS ALMOST HERE YOU GUYS! I'M SO EXCITED!'

WHAT'S YOUR REVIEW?

MAKE FAKE ART GALLERY PLAQUES FOR ALL OF THE STUFF HANGING UP IN YOUR PARENTS' HOUSE.

WHAT'S YOUR REVIEW?

TRY TO GO AN ENTIRE DAY ONLY SAYING
THE WORD 'WHY'—BUT DON'T TELL ANYONE. IF
FIVE-YEAR-OLDS CAN DO IT, YOU CAN TO.

- -
- -
- -
- -
- -
- -
- -
- -
- -
- -

——————— WHAT'S YOUR REVIEW? ———————

EXHIBIT A

**HELP YOUR FAMILY BY PREWRITING YOUR OWN
OBITUARY. INCLUDE PLENTY OF NOTABLE
ACHIEVEMENTS THAT YOU NEVER ACTUALLY DID.**

. . . .

. . . .

. . . .

. . . .

. . . .

. . . .

. . . .

. . . .

. . . .

. . . .

. . . .

. . . .

. . . .

. . . .

. . . .

. . . .

. . . .

. . . .

——— NO PAPER? WELL, YOU'RE IN LUCK. ———

BECOME AN EXTRA IN A MOVIE–EITHER BY SIGNING UP, OR JUST TRYING TO WALK IN FRONT OF CAMERAS WHILE THEY'RE FILMING.

. . . .

. . . .

——————— WHAT'S YOUR REVIEW? ———————

LEARN HOW TO START A FIRE USING ONLY STICKS. IF ALL ELSE FAILS, MATCHES ARE TECHNICALLY STICKS.

. . . .

. . . .

——————— WHAT'S YOUR REVIEW? ———————

GO SHOPPING IN AN IKEA–BUT ONCE YOU GET TIRED, FIND YOUR FAVORITE STAGED ROOM & TAKE A NAP IN ONE OF THE BEDS.

. . . .

. . . .

——————— WHAT'S YOUR REVIEW? ———————

DO ONE OF THOSE RESTAURANT CHALLENGES
WHERE YOU HAVE TO EAT A THREE POUND
STEAK IN AN HOUR TO GET A FREE T-SHIRT.

—— WHAT'S YOUR REVIEW? ——

EXHIBIT A

PARTICIPATE IN A COOKING COMPETITION AND EITHER WIN, OR DO SO HORRIBLY THAT IT'S NOTEWORTHY.

. . . .

. . . .

. . . .

. . . .

. . . .

. . . .

. . . .

. . . .

. . . .

. . . .

——————— WHAT'S YOUR REVIEW? ———————

EXHIBIT A

GET MARRIED IN VEGAS. PRO-TIP: IF YOU
WANT TO SAVE TIME LATER—GO AHEAD AND
GET DIVORCED WHILE YOU'RE AT IT.

WHAT'S YOUR REVIEW?

WRITE THE GREAT AMERICAN NOVEL.
ACTUALLY, IT DOESN'T HAVE TO BE GREAT,
OR EVEN AMERICAN. JUST A NOVEL.

WHAT'S YOUR REVIEW?

GO TO A FANCY RESTAURANT ALONE & ORDER
A 4 COURSE MEAL—INSIST THAT THEY PUT DOWN
ANOTHER PLACE SETTING FOR BRUCE WILLIS.

. . . .

. . . .

. . . .

. . . .

. . . .

. . . .

WHAT'S YOUR REVIEW?

PLAY A GAME OF HOT POTATO—WITH AN
ACTUAL HOT POTATO. BONUS POINTS IF IT'S
COVERED IN BUTTER AND SOUR CREAM.

. . . .

. . . .

. . . .

. . . .

. . . .

. . . .

WHAT'S YOUR REVIEW?

PRETEND YOUR CAMERA IS BROKEN & TRY TO
SELL AN ITEM ONLINE USING ONLY A DRAWING.
BONUS POINTS IF SOMEONE ACTUALLY BUYS IT.

DON'T HAVE A SKETCHBOOK HANDY? USE THIS:

SIGN YOUR MASTERPIECE

EAT AT EVERY SINGLE PIZZA PLACE IN YOUR CITY & RATE THEM TO FINALLY DETERMINE WHICH ONE IS BEST (RIP IF YOU LIVE IN NYC).

. . . .

. . . .

. . . .

. . . .

. . . .

. . . .

. . . .

. . . .

. . . .

. . . .

. . . .

. . . .

. . . .

. . . .

. . . .

. . . .

. . . .

. . . .

. . . .

. . . .

KEEP A RUNNING LIST HERE.

CLIMB MOUNT KILIMANJARO. NOT ALL
OF IT, THAT'S WAY TOO HARD—BUT LIKE, FOR
A GOOD TWENTY FEET.

WHAT'S YOUR REVIEW?

DELIVER THE BEST MAN/MAID OF HONOR
SPEECH AT A WEDDING. THIS WILL GO OVER
BETTER IF YOU WERE INVITED.

WHAT'S YOUR REVIEW?

JOIN THE MILE HIGH CLUB BY EITHER
HAVING SEX IN AN AIRPLANE, OR DENVER,
COLORADO.

WHAT'S YOUR REVIEW?

LEARN SIGN LANGUAGE. NATURALLY, START WITH THE CURSE WORDS AND JUST EXPAND FROM THERE.

WHAT'S YOUR REVIEW?

DRINK A WHISKEY FROM THE YEAR THAT YOU WERE BORN. NEAT. OH, AND YOU SHOULD DRINK IT WITHOUT ICE.

WHAT'S YOUR REVIEW?

SING KARAOKE WITH YOUR BEST FRIEND. ALSO, GET DRUNK ENOUGH TO ACTUALLY SING KARAOKE WITH YOUR BEST FRIEND.

WHAT'S YOUR REVIEW?

EXHIBIT A

BE THE BACK HALF OF A TWO PERSON HORSE COSTUME—JUST BE SURE TO CHOOSE YOUR PARTNER (AND THEIR DIET) WISELY.

WHAT'S YOUR REVIEW?

EXHIBIT A

RAISE A THOUSAND DOLLARS FOR A CHARITY THAT YOU CARE ABOUT. HEY, THIS ISN'T ALL JUST FUN AND GAMES.

WHAT'S YOUR REVIEW?

WATCH YOUR PARENTS' FAVORITE MOVIES—WITH THEM IF THEY'RE ALIVE, OR WITH THEIR GHOSTS IF THEY AREN'T.

WHAT'S YOUR REVIEW?

SEE A BASEBALL GAME IN EVERY MAJOR LEAGUE STADIUM—AND GET ON THE JUMBOTRON AT LEAST ONCE.

WHAT'S YOUR REVIEW?

EXHIBIT A

SPEND A NIGHT IN JAIL. IT'S DEALER'S
CHOICE ON HOW YOU GET THERE THOUGH.
HAVE FUN WITH IT.

WHAT'S YOUR REVIEW?

TAKE SOME OLD CLOTHES FROM HOME &
REDRESS A MANNEQUIN AT YOUR LOCAL MALL.
JUST ACT LIKE IT'S YOUR JOB—SIGH A LOT.

WHAT'S YOUR REVIEW?

ATTEND AN IN-PERSON AUCTION AND
CONFIDENTLY BID ON SOMETHING THAT YOU
CAN'T AFFORD—THEN PRAY TO BE OUTBID.

. . . .

. . . .

. . . .

. . . .

. . . .

. . . .

——— WHAT'S YOUR REVIEW? ———

BEFRIEND A CROW, AND TEACH
IT TO BRING YOU SHINY THINGS IN
EXCHANGE FOR SNACKS.

. . . .

. . . .

. . . .

. . . .

. . . .

. . . .

——— WHAT'S YOUR REVIEW? ———

GET A TATTOO OF YOUR FAVORITE BREAKFAST
CEREAL. SKETCH OUT A FEW IDEAS FIRST
THOUGH—DON'T RUSH SUCH A BIG DECISION.

DON'T HAVE A CANVAS HANDY? USE THIS:

SIGN YOUR MASTERPIECE

EAT AS MANY DIFFERENT SPECIES OF ANIMALS
AS YOU CAN & KEEP A LIST. VEGETARIAN? LIST
SOME VARIETIES OF CARROTS OR WHATEVER.

BECOME A MILLIONAIRE. ACTUALLY, YOU MIGHT WANT TO DO THIS ONE FIRST—IT WILL MAKE THE REST WAY EASIER.

. . . .

. . . .

. . . .

. . . .

. . . .

. . . .

———— WHAT'S YOUR REVIEW? ————

FLY FIRST CLASS TO ANOTHER COUNTRY—AND RUIN ALL FUTURE AIR TRAVEL FOR YOURSELF.

. . . .

. . . .

. . . .

. . . .

. . . .

. . . .

———— WHAT'S YOUR REVIEW? ————

**HIRE A MARIACHI BAND TO FOLLOW
YOU EVERYWHERE YOU GO FOR AN ENTIRE
DAY—LIKE THE GROCERY STORE.**

WHAT'S YOUR REVIEW?

**EAT FRENCH FRIES IN FRANCE, OR
EAT SUBWAY IN THE SUBWAY.**

WHAT'S YOUR REVIEW?

**ADOPT A PENGUIN, BUT GET REALLY
MAD WHEN YOU FIND OUT THAT THEY DON'T
ACTUALLY MAIL YOU A PENGUIN.**

WHAT'S YOUR REVIEW?

SIGN UP TO DRIVE A REAL NASCAR—BUT WHEN IT'S YOUR TURN BEHIND THE WHEEL, GO AS SLOW AS POSSIBLE. MAKE IT LAST.

WHAT'S YOUR REVIEW?

EXHIBIT A

GET A PERM. LIKE, ON PURPOSE. NOW DRAW SOME BEFORE AND AFTER SELF-PORTRAITS.

DON'T HAVE A CANVAS HANDY? USE THIS:

SIGN YOUR MASTERPIECE

TURN YOUR PHONE OFF FOR AN ENTIRE
WEEK. PRO-TIP: LET OTHER PEOPLE KNOW
FIRST, BEFORE THEY THINK YOU DIED.

WHAT'S YOUR REVIEW?

BE PART OF A FLASH MOB—RIGHT AFTER
YOU TIME TRAVEL BACK TO 2007 WHEN THEY
WERE STILL A THING.

WHAT'S YOUR REVIEW?

PLAY POKER IN A CASINO & SUCCESSFULLY MANAGE TO NOT LOSE ALL YOUR MONEY IN THE FIRST FIVE MINUTES.

— WHAT'S YOUR REVIEW? —

EXHIBIT A

DRESS UP LIKE A HUNCHBACK AND GO ON A COLLEGE ADMISSIONS TOUR OF NOTRE DAME.

. . . .
. . . .

——— WHAT'S YOUR REVIEW? ———

GO ON AN INTERVIEW & ONLY ANSWER THEIR QUESTIONS WITH SONG LYRICS. STRENGTHS? 'I GET KNOCKED DOWN, BUT I GET UP AGAIN.'

. . . .
. . . .

——— WHAT'S YOUR REVIEW? ———

ATTEND A MURDER MYSTERY DINNER, AND EVEN THOUGH IT WOULD BE THE PERFECT PLACE TO KILL SOMEONE—RESIST THE URGE.

. . . .
. . . .

——— WHAT'S YOUR REVIEW? ———

EARN A BLACK BELT IN KARATE.
OR EARN A BLACK BELT AT KOHL'S. HEY,
THAT KOHL'S CASH REALLY ADDS UP.

· ·

· ·

· ·

· ·

· ·

· ·

WHAT'S YOUR REVIEW?

WIPE YOUR BUTT WITH A DOLLAR & FEEL
LIKE JEFF BEZOS—IF ONLY FOR A SECOND, UNTIL
YOU REALIZE YOU NOW HAVE A POO DOLLAR.

· ·

· ·

· ·

· ·

· ·

· ·

WHAT'S YOUR REVIEW?

SPEND A YEAR LIVING IN EUROPE—UNLESS YOU ALREADY LIVE IN EUROPE. THEN SPEND A YEAR GLOATING ABOUT HOW GREAT IT IS.

. . . .
. . . .
. . . .
. . . .
. . . .
. . . .

——————— WHAT'S YOUR REVIEW? ———————

EAT A DONUT WHILE SITTING IN A POLICE CAR—PREFERABLY IN ONE OF THE FRONT SEATS.

. . . .
. . . .
. . . .
. . . .
. . . .
. . . .

——————— WHAT'S YOUR REVIEW? ———————

INSTEAD OF CALLING IN SICK, HIRE A SINGING
TELEGRAM TO LET YOUR BOSS KNOW. BONUS IF
THEY CAN RHYME WITH DIARRHEA.

WHAT'S YOUR REVIEW?

EXHIBIT A

MAKE A LIST OF EVERY SO-CALLED GREAT ALBUM THAT YOU'VE NEVER HEARD & LISTEN TO THEM ALL—NO MATTER HOW OVERRATED.

. . . .

. . . .

. . . .

. . . .

. . . .

. . . .

. . . .

. . . .

. . . .

. . . .

. . . .

. . . .

. . . .

. . . .

. . . .

. . . .

. . . .

. . . .

. . . .

. . . .

——————— NO PAPER? WELL, YOU'RE IN LUCK. ———————

RUN FOR LOCAL OFFICE – IDEALLY SOMETHING THAT YOU WON'T SCREW UP TOO BADLY, BUT NOT LIKE THAT'S STOPPED ANYONE ELSE.

. . . .
. . . .

———— WHAT'S YOUR REVIEW? ————

DRIVE THE ENTIRETY OF ROUTE 66, GOING FROM CHICAGO TO SAN DIEGO – ESPECIALLY IF YOU LIKE LOOKING AT ABANDONED MOTELS.

. . . .
. . . .

———— WHAT'S YOUR REVIEW? ————

STAND AT THE FRONT OF A BOAT & DO THAT 'I'M KING OF THE WORLD' THING – WHILE YOUR DAD IS JUST TRYING TO FISH.

. . . .
. . . .

———— WHAT'S YOUR REVIEW? ————

SING YOUR ORDER AT A MCDONALD'S DRIVE THRU—BUT JUST READ IT OFF AFTER THEY APPLAUD AND/OR SAY 'WHAT?'

. . . .

. . . .

. . . .

. . . .

. . . .

. . . .

. . . .

. . . .

. . . .

. . . .

——————— WHAT'S YOUR REVIEW? ———————

EXHIBIT A

GO VIRAL ON THE INTERNET. ADMITTEDLY
THIS ONE IS WAY HARDER THAN JUST BEING
HIGHLY CONTAGIOUS IN REAL LIFE.

— WHAT'S YOUR REVIEW? —

EXHIBIT A

EARN YOUR PERSONAL PILOT LICENSE. IF
IT SEEMS TOO DIFFICULT, JUST REMEMBER:
JOHN TRAVOLTA.

WHAT'S YOUR REVIEW?

EAT RAW OYSTERS RIGHT OUT OF THE
SHELL—AS OPPOSED TO RIGHT OFF OF
THE FLOOR, I GUESS?

WHAT'S YOUR REVIEW?

SELL SOMEONE YOUR SOUL.
OR BUY SOMEONE ELSE'S!

WHAT'S YOUR REVIEW?

GET A SPEEDING TICKET, AND THEN TRY TO TALK YOUR WAY OUT OF IT—BUT YOU PROBABLY SHOULDN'T SHOW THE OFFICER THIS BOOK.

WHAT'S YOUR REVIEW?

DRAW A PORTRAIT OF YOUR FAVORITE
CELEBRITY & SEND IT TO THEM ON TWITTER.
NOW HARASS THEM UNTIL THEY RETWEET IT.

DON'T HAVE A CANVAS HANDY? USE THIS:

SIGN YOUR MASTERPIECE

WRITE DOWN THE PLAYLIST FOR YOUR FUTURE FUNERAL—BUT IF YOU DON'T INCLUDE "STAYIN' ALIVE" YOU'RE DOING IT WRONG.

HIKE TO THE TOP OF A VOLCANO—FOR BEST RESULTS, CHOOSE ONE THAT ISN'T CURRENTLY ACTIVE.

WHAT'S YOUR REVIEW?

GET A SANDWICH NAMED AFTER YOU AT A LOCAL DELI—A GOOD ONE, NOT SOME BOLOGNA BULLSHIT.

WHAT'S YOUR REVIEW?

BRIBE A MEMBER OF CONGRESS. JUST SLIP THEM FIVE BUCKS AND SAY 'YOU NEVER SAW ME HERE.'

WHAT'S YOUR REVIEW?

WALK ACROSS ABBEY ROAD IN LONDON AND LOUDLY ASK 'WHY ARE THERE SO MANY PEOPLE LOOKING AT SOME STREET?!'

. . . .

. . . .

. . . .

. . . .

. . . .

. . . .

—————— WHAT'S YOUR REVIEW? ——————

MAKE YOUR OWN BUCKET LIST. MEANING BUY A REALLY NICE BUCKET AND WRITE YOUR TO-DO LIST ON IT.

. . . .

. . . .

. . . .

. . . .

. . . .

. . . .

—————— WHAT'S YOUR REVIEW? ——————

THROW A GLASS OF WATER IN SOMEONE'S FACE IN THE MIDDLE OF A RESTAURANT. NOT OUT OF ANGER—JUST BECAUSE.

----------------- WHAT'S YOUR REVIEW? -----------------

EXHIBIT A

FIND SOMEBODY ELSE THAT HAS YOUR EXACT SAME FIRST & LAST NAME AND TAKE THEM OUT TO LUNCH.

——————— WHAT'S YOUR REVIEW? ———————

EXHIBIT A

LEARN HOW TO EAT FIRE, OR AT LEAST ORDER SOME OF THAT REALLY AWESOME FLAMING CHEESE STUFF.

PSST: IT'S CALLED RACLETTE, AND IT'S DELICIOUS.

. . . .

. . . .

. . . .

. . . .

. . . .

. . . .

——————— WHAT'S YOUR REVIEW? ———————

START YOUR OWN CULT. OR YOU COULD JOIN ONE—BUT JOINING CULTS IS FOR SUCKERS.

. . . .

. . . .

. . . .

. . . .

. . . .

. . . .

——————— WHAT'S YOUR REVIEW? ———————

HAVE YOUR HANDWRITING ANALYZED TO REVEAL
HIDDEN PERSONALITY TRAITS—BUT IF YOU PUT
HEARTS OVER I'S YOU'RE CLEARLY A PSYCHOPATH.

GO TO A DRAG SHOW...OR GO DRAG
RACING...OR JUST MAKE A WHOLE DAY
OF IT AND DO BOTH.

. . . .
. . . .

———— WHAT'S YOUR REVIEW? ————

FIND YOUR OLD PHOTO ALBUM FROM
WHEN YOU WERE A BABY, AND RECREATE EVERY
PHOTO—NO MATTER WHAT.

. . . .
. . . .

———— WHAT'S YOUR REVIEW? ————

TRY TO CATCH A GREASED PIG—BUT IT'LL BE
MORE CHALLENGING TO FIND A FARMER THAT'S
OK WITH YOU GREASING UP THEIR PIG.

. . . .
. . . .

———— WHAT'S YOUR REVIEW? ————

HAVE SOMEONE PAINT A NUDE PORTRAIT OF
YOU & HANG IT ABOVE YOUR MANTLE WITHOUT
EVER ACKNOWLEDGING IT.

WHAT'S YOUR REVIEW?

BECOME FRIENDS WITH THE MANAGER OF
A GROCERY STORE SOLELY TO TALK THEM INTO
LETTING YOU MAKE DUMB ANNOUNCEMENTS.

WHAT'S YOUR REVIEW?

FILL A BOX UP WITH $100 IN PENNIES, BURY
IT SOMEWHERE, & DRAW OUT A TREASURE MAP
TO ENCLOSE IN YOUR WILL.

DON'T HAVE A CANVAS HANDY? USE THIS:

SIGN YOUR MASTERPIECE

START BREWING YOUR OWN BEER—BUT CLASS IT UP & HAND DRAW LABELS TO GLUE ON THE BOTTLES THAT YOU GIVE AWAY.

DON'T HAVE A CANVAS HANDY? USE THIS:

SIGN YOUR MASTERPIECE

WALK BAREFOOT ACROSS A BED OF HOT COALS—BUT IF YOU HAVE EVER STEPPED ON A LEGO, THAT COUNTS TOO.

. . . .

. . . .

. . . .

. . . .

. . . .

. . . .

——————— WHAT'S YOUR REVIEW? ———————

PURPOSEFULLY DO SOMETHING TO EMBARRASS YOURSELF. LIKE, GO ON A GUIDED SEGWAY TOUR OR SOMETHING.

. . . .

. . . .

. . . .

. . . .

. . . .

. . . .

——————— WHAT'S YOUR REVIEW? ———————

SEND YOUR DAD A POSTCARD FROM EVERY HARD ROCK CAFE IN THE COUNTRY. HE'LL BE SO JEALOUS.

. . . .
. . . .

WHAT'S YOUR REVIEW?

FINALLY SIGN UP FOR YOUR FREE 100 HOURS OF AOL. LET'S SEE WHAT ALL THE FUSS IS ABOUT.

. . . .
. . . .

WHAT'S YOUR REVIEW?

INSTEAD OF SELLING YOUR OLD USED CAR, SIGN UP FOR A DEMOLITION DERBY—SPRAY PAINT FLAMES ON THE SIDE, FOR INTIMIDATION.

. . . .
. . . .

WHAT'S YOUR REVIEW?

BREAK A GUINNESS WORLD RECORD—LIKE MOST SMARTIES EATEN IN 60 SECONDS BLINDFOLDED USING CHOPSTICKS. JUST BEAT 20.*

*AT THE TIME OF PRINTING ANYWAY.

WHAT'S YOUR REVIEW?

EXHIBIT A

**GO AHEAD AND WRITE DOWN SOME OPTIONS
FOR YOUR LAST WORDS—THAT WAY IN THE END
YOU'LL JUST HAVE TO POINT.**

. . . .

. . . .

. . . .

. . . .

. . . .

. . . .

. . . .

. . . .

. . . .

. . . .

. . . .

. . . .

. . . .

. . . .

. . . .

. . . .

. . . .

. . . .

——— NO PAPER? WELL, YOU'RE IN LUCK. ———

SPOIL THE END OF A MOVIE
FOR SOMEONE THAT YOU CAN'T STAND.
LIKE VLADIMIR PUTIN.

WHAT'S YOUR REVIEW?

GO TO A RESTAURANT WHERE YOU DON'T
SPEAK THE LANGUAGE & JUST ORDER THINGS AT
RANDOM WITHOUT KNOWING WHAT THEY ARE.*

*UNLESS YOU HAVE ANY SERIOUS ALLERGIES OF COURSE.

WHAT'S YOUR REVIEW?

READ A BOOK FROM ALL 100 DIVISIONS OF THE
DEWEY DECIMAL SYSTEM. PRO-TIP: CHECK OUT
306.73 – THAT'S WHERE THE JUICY STUFF IS.

WHAT'S YOUR REVIEW?

EXHIBIT A

GO TO YOUR LOCAL OLIVE GARDEN AND PUT THOSE 'NEVER ENDING BREADSTICKS' TO THE TEST.

. . . .
. . . .

——————— WHAT'S YOUR REVIEW? ———————

BECOME AN ORDAINED MINISTER ONLINE AT THE UNIVERSAL LIFE CHURCH, AND OFFICIATE SOMEONE'S WEDDING.

. . . .
. . . .

——————— WHAT'S YOUR REVIEW? ———————

FOLLOW YOUR FAVORITE BAND FOR THEIR ENTIRE TOUR. HEY, YOU SHOULD EVEN GO TO ONE OF THE CONCERTS!

. . . .
. . . .

——————— WHAT'S YOUR REVIEW? ———————

RENT OUT A BILLBOARD FOR A MONTH,
BUT JUST PUT UP A PICTURE OF YOUR FACE,
THE WORD 'HI,' AND NO EXPLANATION.

WHAT'S YOUR REVIEW?

WATCH THE NYE BALL DROP IN TIMES
SQUARE – ON TV. UNLESS YOU LIKE WEARING A
DIAPER, THEN KNOCK YOURSELF OUT I GUESS.

WHAT'S YOUR REVIEW?

PACK YOUR SUITCASE, HEAD TO THE TRAIN STATION, AND TAKE THE NEXT ONE GOING ANYWHERE. VOILÁ—RANDOM VACATION!

. . . .

. . . .

. . . .

. . . .

. . . .

. . . .

———— WHAT'S YOUR REVIEW? ————

HAVE A BAR WHERE EVERYBODY KNOWS YOUR NAME—WHILE ALSO MANAGING TO NOT DEVELOP A DRINKING PROBLEM.

. . . .

. . . .

. . . .

. . . .

. . . .

. . . .

———— WHAT'S YOUR REVIEW? ————

READ A BIOGRAPHY OF EVERY U.S. PRESIDENT.
EVEN WILLIAM HARRISON—ALTHOUGH THE BOOK
COULD TAKE LONGER THAN HIS PRESIDENCY.

WHAT'S YOUR REVIEW?

EXHIBIT A

WRITE DOWN THE RECIPE OF YOUR FAVORITE MEAL & GIVE IT TO ALL OF YOUR FRIENDS—ON THE CONDITION THAT THEY MAKE IT FOR YOU.

HAVE SEX IN ALL 50 STATES—AND PUERTO RICO, JUST IN CASE THAT STATEHOOD THING EVER HAPPENS.

. . . .
. . . .

———— WHAT'S YOUR REVIEW? ————

GET INTERVIEWED BY THE LOCAL NEWS DURING A LIVE SEGMENT—BUT JUST FREEZE UP & DON'T SAY A WORD UNTIL THEY CUT AWAY.

. . . .
. . . .

———— WHAT'S YOUR REVIEW? ————

MEET UP W/ PEOPLE THAT YOU ONLY KNOW FROM THE INTERNET. IT'S FINALLY TIME TO SEE WHAT 'WHEATTHICKS27' IS LIKE IN PERSON.

. . . .
. . . .

———— WHAT'S YOUR REVIEW? ————

STAY IN A HOSTEL AND FINALLY FIND OUT IF THEY ARE TRULY AS ENJOYABLE AS THE NAME IMPLIES.

—————————————— WHAT'S YOUR REVIEW? ——————————————

EXHIBIT A

ENROLL IN CLOWN COLLEGE – BUT DROP OUT AFTER A WEEK. TELL THEM THAT 'YOU'RE JUST JUGGLING TOO MUCH RIGHT NOW.'

. . . .

. . . .

. . . .

. . . .

. . . .

. . . .

. . . .

. . . .

. . . .

. . . .

———— WHAT'S YOUR REVIEW? ————

EXHIBIT A

TAKE THE CLICHÉ PHOTO OF YOU HOLDING UP THE LEANING TOWER OF PISA—BUT PURPOSELY USE THE WRONG BUILDING.

WHAT'S YOUR REVIEW?

KISS SOMEONE AT MIDNIGHT ON NEW YEAR'S EVE—BEFORE YOU GET OLD ENOUGH TO REALIZE THAT NEW YEAR'S IS THE WORST.

WHAT'S YOUR REVIEW?

TAKE A CROSS-COUNTRY TRIP IN AN RV—THAT
SHOULD FINALLY MAKE YOU APPRECIATE THE
INVENTION OF AIR TRAVEL.

. . . .

. . . .

. . . .

. . . .

. . . .

. . . .

————————— WHAT'S YOUR REVIEW? —————————

SPEND THE NIGHT IN A HAUNTED
MANSION—OR A HAUNTED MCMANSION IF
YOU LIVE IN THE SUBURBS.

. . . .

. . . .

. . . .

. . . .

. . . .

. . . .

————————— WHAT'S YOUR REVIEW? —————————

DRAW YOUR FAMILY, DATE IT, & HIDE IT IN YOUR
HOUSE FOR A FUTURE OWNER—ADD A PHOTO TOO,
SO THEY'LL KNOW HOW BAD YOU WERE AT ART.

DON'T HAVE A CANVAS HANDY? USE THIS:

SIGN YOUR MASTERPIECE

INVENT YOUR OWN SIGNATURE COCKTAIL—NOW GIVE IT A WEIRD NAME AND TRY TO GET IT TO CATCH ON.*

*WE'LL HELP. SEND IT TO US @BRASSMONKEYGOODS

. . . .

. . . .

. . . .

. . . .

. . . .

. . . .

. . . .

. . . .

. . . .

. . . .

. . . .

. . . .

. . . .

. . . .

. . . .

. . . .

. . . .

——— WRITE DOWN THE RECIPE, FOR POSTERITY ———

SLEEP OUT UNDER THE STARS—IDEALLY
ON PURPOSE, AND NOT JUST BECAUSE YOU
LOCKED YOURSELF OUT.

WHAT'S YOUR REVIEW?

**SMOKE POT WITH YOUR PARENTS AND/OR
WILLIE NELSON—WHICHEVER IS MORE LIKELY
TO HAPPEN.**

WHAT'S YOUR REVIEW?

GO TO HELL.
SPECIFICALLY HELL, MICHIGAN.
IT'S BEAUTIFUL IN THE FALL.

WHAT'S YOUR REVIEW?

WORK AT A RENAISSANCE FESTIVAL—WHICH IS BASICALLY JUST WALKING AROUND IN TIGHTS, EATING TURKEY LEGS, & YELLING 'HUZZAH.'

. . . .

. . . .

. . . .

. . . .

. . . .

. . . .

——— WHAT'S YOUR REVIEW? ———

GO SKINNY DIPPING IN A LAKE—BUT IT'S UP TO YOU IF YOU WANT TO INVITE OTHER PEOPLE OR NOT.

. . . .

. . . .

. . . .

. . . .

. . . .

. . . .

——— WHAT'S YOUR REVIEW? ———

ENTER INTO A HOT DOG EATING CONTEST—PRIMARILY JUST FOR ALL OF THE FREE HOT DOGS.

....

....

....

....

....

....

....

....

....

....

——— WHAT'S YOUR REVIEW? ———

EXHIBIT A

JOIN IN ON A DRUM CIRCLE—AND DON'T
WORRY ABOUT BEING GOOD AT IT. TRUST US,
NONE OF THE OTHER PEOPLE ARE EITHER.

WHAT'S YOUR REVIEW?

EXHIBIT A

GO TO OKTOBERFEST IN MUNICH, GERMANY. FUN CHALLENGE: ASK THEM IF THEY HAVE ANY O'DOUL'S & TRY NOT TO BE MURDERED.

WHAT'S YOUR REVIEW?

PROACTIVELY DO SOMETHING NICE FOR A COMPLETE STRANGER—BTW, WE COUNT AS STRANGERS...AND WE LOVE COOKIES.

1107 HICKORY STREET • KANSAS CITY, MO 64101 • YOU KNOW, JUST IN CASE.

WHAT'S YOUR REVIEW?

BE A CONTESTANT ON 'THE PRICE IS RIGHT,' AND BID $1—FOR EVERYTHING, EVEN THE SHOWCASE SHOWDOWN.

WHAT'S YOUR REVIEW?

TOUCH A BOOB THAT ISN'T YOUR OWN. WITH PERMISSION OF COURSE.

SERIOUSLY, DON'T BE CREEPY.

WHAT'S YOUR REVIEW?

TAKE A TOUR OF AN ALLIGATOR FARM—AND REPEATEDLY ASK HOW THEY GO ABOUT HARVESTING THEM.

WHAT'S YOUR REVIEW?

GO TO AN AXE-THROWING BAR AND REFUSE
TO LEAVE UNTIL YOU GET A BULLSEYE—OR
LOSE ALL FEELING IN YOUR ARM.

· ·

· ·

· ·

· ·

· ·

· ·

——————— WHAT'S YOUR REVIEW? ———————

ENTER YOUR VEHICLE INTO A
CAR SHOW—EVEN IF IT'S A 2003
TOYOTA COROLLA.

· ·

· ·

· ·

· ·

· ·

· ·

——————— WHAT'S YOUR REVIEW? ———————

LEARN A SECOND LANGUAGE—WHILE ALSO CURSING YOUR PARENTS FOR NOT FORCING YOU TO DO IT AGAINST YOUR WILL AS A KID.

WHAT'S YOUR REVIEW?

RIDE EVERY SINGLE ROLLER COASTER AT A THEME PARK IN 1 DAY—INCLUDING ANY KIDDIE ONES THAT THEY'LL STILL LET YOU GET ON.

WHAT'S YOUR REVIEW?

PLAY ROAD TRIP BINGO WITH YOUR NEXT
CAB DRIVER—SO MAKE A LIST OF EASY THINGS
TO SPOT, LIKE STICK-FIGURE FAMILY DECALS.

MAKE A LIST OF EVERYONE THAT YOU'RE LOOKING FORWARD TO HAUNTING—AND HOW YOU'LL DO IT.

PUT A TEMPORARY TATTOO ON YOUR FACE & GO VISIT YOUR GRANDPARENTS FOR THANKSGIVING DINNER.

. . . .

. . . .

. . . .

. . . .

. . . .

. . . .

—————— WHAT'S YOUR REVIEW? ——————

POST VIDEOS OF YOURSELF DOING SOMETHING YOU'RE REALLY GOOD AT ON YOUTUBE—AND NEVER, EVER LOOK AT THE COMMENTS.

. . . .

. . . .

. . . .

. . . .

. . . .

. . . .

—————— WHAT'S YOUR REVIEW? ——————

LIVE IN AN APARTMENT? BECOME FRIENDS W/ THE UPSTAIRS NEIGHBORS OF YOUR UPSTAIRS NEIGHBORS & START A RIVER DANCING CLUB.

. . . .

. . . .

. . . .

. . . .

. . . .

. . . .

———— WHAT'S YOUR REVIEW? ————

KISS SOMEONE YOU LOVE IN THE MIDDLE OF THE POURING RAIN—BECAUSE IT'S SUPER ROMANTIC TO BE REALLY COLD & WET.

. . . .

. . . .

. . . .

. . . .

. . . .

. . . .

———— WHAT'S YOUR REVIEW? ————

GO ICE FISHING IN THE MIDDLE OF A FROZEN LAKE. ALSO, FIGURE OUT HOW TO GO TO THE BATHROOM IN THE MIDDLE OF A FROZEN LAKE.

. . . .

. . . .

———— WHAT'S YOUR REVIEW? ————

VISIT THE FOUR CORNERS AND STAND IN FOUR KIND OF BORING STATES—BUT ALL AT ONE TIME!

. . . .

. . . .

———— WHAT'S YOUR REVIEW? ————

EAT SOME FRIED CRICKETS—TRY COVERING THEM IN CHOCOLATE FOR THE DECADENT TREAT THAT NO ONE EVER WANTED TO BEGIN WITH.

. . . .

. . . .

———— WHAT'S YOUR REVIEW? ————

JUMP OUT OF A PLANE WHILE YELLING 'GERONIMO!' & SIMULTANEOUSLY GOOGLING 'WHY DO PEOPLE YELL GERONIMO?'

....

....

....

....

....

....

....

....

....

....

—————— WHAT'S YOUR REVIEW? ——————

EXHIBIT A

DESIGN YOUR FUTURE TOMBSTONE—THE SKY IS THE LIMIT. MAYBE SOMETHING CLASSY, LIKE CALVIN PEEING ON THE GRIM REAPER.

DON'T HAVE A CANVAS HANDY? USE THIS:

SIGN YOUR MASTERPIECE

GET HYPNOTIZED ON STAGE. BE SURE TO
HAVE SOMEONE FILM IT, BECAUSE YOU'LL NEED
TO KNOW WHAT TO BE EMBARRASSED ABOUT.

. . . .

. . . .

. . . .

. . . .

. . . .

. . . .

——————— WHAT'S YOUR REVIEW? ———————

TRY DRINKING ABSINTHE. SPOILER ALERT:
ALL OF THAT HALLUCINOGENIC STUFF IS A
LIE—IT'LL JUST GET YOU PRETTY DRUNK.

. . . .

. . . .

. . . .

. . . .

. . . .

. . . .

——————— WHAT'S YOUR REVIEW? ———————

RUN THE FIRST HALF OF A 10K, THEN STOP
IN THE ROAD FOR A PICNIC. FINISH THE RACE
AFTER YOU'VE DIGESTED A BIT.

WHAT'S YOUR REVIEW?

EXHIBIT A

**PLAY THE LOTTERY. NEED SOME NUMBERS?
01 • 09 • 23 • 26 • 44 + 10 FOR THE BONUS.
YOU BETTER SPLIT IT IF YOU WIN THOUGH.**

. . . .
. . . .

WHAT'S YOUR REVIEW?

**EAT A DEEP DISH PIZZA IN CHICAGO,
A CHEESESTEAK IN PHILADELPHIA, AND
A CAN OF SPAM IN HAWAII.**

. . . .
. . . .

WHAT'S YOUR REVIEW?

**ATTEND THE BURNING MAN FESTIVAL—BUT
MAYBE ONLY IF YOU'VE LOST YOUR SENSE OF
SMELL IN A FREAK ACCIDENT OR SOMETHING.**

. . . .
. . . .

WHAT'S YOUR REVIEW?

GO SPELUNKING IN A CAVE. AND NO, THAT'S NOT A EUPHEMISM FOR POOPING.

WHAT'S YOUR REVIEW?

PLAY DUNGEONS AND DRAGONS FOR THE FIRST TIME WITH PEOPLE THAT LOVE IT & JUST MARVEL AT HOW ANGRY THEY GET AT YOU.

WHAT'S YOUR REVIEW?

WATCH THE GODFATHER TRILOGY, OR THE POLICE ACADEMY HEPTALOGY—DEPENDING ON YOUR DEFINITION OF FINE CINEMA.

. . . .

. . . .

. . . .

. . . .

. . . .

. . . .

——— WHAT'S YOUR REVIEW? ———

NEXT TIME YOU GET PULLED OVER, HAND THE OFFICER AN OLD MONOPOLY 'GET OUT OF JAIL FREE' CARD & SAY 'I THINK WE'RE DONE HERE.'

. . . .

. . . .

. . . .

. . . .

. . . .

. . . .

——— WHAT'S YOUR REVIEW? ———

START PLAYING TIC-TAC-TOE WITH YOUR
MAIL CARRIER. MAKE THE FIRST MOVE AND
TAPE IT TO YOUR MAILBOX.

DON'T HAVE ANY PAPER HANDY? USE THIS:

BEST OUT OF ELEVEN WINS

CATCH, COOK, CLEAN, AND EAT YOUR OWN FISH. MEANING A FISH FROM A LAKE—NOT YOUR GOLDFISH OR SOMETHING.

. . . .

. . . .

. . . .

. . . .

. . . .

. . . .

. . . .

. . . .

. . . .

. . . .

——————— WHAT'S YOUR REVIEW? ———————

EXHIBIT A

ASK SOMEONE TO WRITE
A POEM ABOUT YOU, OR EVEN
BETTER, A LIMERICK.

LEARN HOW TO KNIT—BY MAKING COUNTLESS TERRIBLE SCARVES & GUILTING YOUR FRIENDS AND FAMILY INTO WEARING THEM.

. . . .
. . . .

———— WHAT'S YOUR REVIEW? ————

HAVE PHONE SEX WITH SOMEONE. OR WATCH 'HER' AND SEE SOMEONE HAVE SEX WITH A PHONE.*

*SORRY FOR THE CIRCA. 2017 SPOILER.

. . . .
. . . .

———— WHAT'S YOUR REVIEW? ————

PUT UP SOME 'MISSING' POSTERS AROUND TOWN WITH YOUR FACE ON THEM AND SEE HOW LONG IT TAKES SOMEONE TO FIND YOU.

. . . .
. . . .

———— WHAT'S YOUR REVIEW? ————

SING THE NATIONAL ANTHEM AT A SPORTING EVENT—EVEN IF NO ONE ACTUALLY ASKED YOU TO.

————— WHAT'S YOUR REVIEW? —————

EXHIBIT A

GO TO THE DELI COUNTER OF YOUR LOCAL STORE & BUY THE LARGEST CHEESE WHEEL. NOT SLICED—JUST ROLL IT UP TO THE CHECKOUT.

WHAT'S YOUR REVIEW?

EXHIBIT A

BORN AFTER THE YEAR 2000? GO INSIDE OF A LIBRARY AND SEE WHAT LIFE WAS LIKE BEFORE THE INTERNET.

. . . .

. . . .

. . . .

. . . .

. . . .

. . . .

———— WHAT'S YOUR REVIEW? ————

WRITE AND RECORD AN ORIGINAL SONG, NO MATTER HOW TERRIBLE IT IS—AT THE VERY LEAST YOU CAN USE IT TO KEEP RACCOONS AWAY.

. . . .

. . . .

. . . .

. . . .

. . . .

. . . .

———— WHAT'S YOUR REVIEW? ————

HAVE A MÉNAGE À TROIS, WHICH IS PROBABLY
A LOT LIKE A CRÈME BRÛLÉE—BUT I'D LOOK IT
UP BEFORE YOU ASK FOR ONE AT DENNY'S.

WHAT'S YOUR REVIEW?

WALK UP TO A STRANGER ON THE STREET, TAP
THEM ON THE SHOULDER, & YELL 'TAG, YOU'RE
IT!'—NOW RUN AWAY AS FAST AS YOU CAN.

WHAT'S YOUR REVIEW?

TAKE A NUDE FIGURE DRAWING CLASS. BE SURE TO ADD IT TO YOUR LINKEDIN PROFILE UNDER EDUCATION—EVEN IF YOU'RE AN ACCOUNTANT.

DON'T HAVE A CANVAS HANDY? USE THIS:

SIGN YOUR MASTERPIECE

MAKE A LIST OF ALL THE MOVIES THAT YOU'VE SEEN THAT WERE A WASTE OF MONEY—NOW WRITE TO EACH STUDIO AND DEMAND A REFUND.

· ·

· ·

· ·

· ·

· ·

· ·

· ·

· ·

· ·

· ·

· ·

· ·

· ·

· ·

· ·

· ·

· ·

· ·

· ·

· ·

· ·

——— NO PAPER? WELL, YOU'RE IN LUCK. ———

BUY THE BIGGEST PIÑATA THAT YOU
CAN FIND, FILL IT WITH CANDY, AND HANG
IT UP IN A RANDOM SUBWAY CAR.

WHAT'S YOUR REVIEW?

DRESS UP LIKE SANTA AND SEE HOW
MANY ADULTS YOU CAN GET TO SIT ON
YOUR LAP—IN MARCH.

WHAT'S YOUR REVIEW?

TAKE A PHOTO OF YOURSELF EVERY DAY WHEN
YOU GET TO WORK & MAKE A TIME LAPSE VIDEO
W/ THEM. ALSO, SORRY FOR THE BUMMER.

WHAT'S YOUR REVIEW?

TEACH AN OLD DOG A NEW TRICK. IF ALL ELSE FAILS, WORK ON 'LAY DOWN.' THEY SHOULD BE ABLE TO HANDLE THAT ONE.

. . . .
. . . .
. . . .
. . . .
. . . .
. . . .

—————— WHAT'S YOUR REVIEW? ——————

GO MOREL MUSHROOM HUNTING WHILE EATING MUSHROOMS. LIKE PORTOBELLOS. WAIT, WHAT DID YOU THINK WE MEANT?

. . . .
. . . .
. . . .
. . . .
. . . .
. . . .

—————— WHAT'S YOUR REVIEW? ——————

PAY FOR A LARGE PURCHASE ENTIRELY IN PENNIES. LIKE AN APPLIANCE, OR A CAR, OR A 30 YEAR MORTGAGE.

. . . .
. . . .
. . . .
. . . .
. . . .
. . . .
. . . .
. . . .
. . . .
. . . .

——— WHAT'S YOUR REVIEW? ———

EXHIBIT A

LEARN HOW TO YODEL & ACQUIRE A USEFUL LIFE SKILL—BEING ABLE TO END ANY AWKWARD CONVERSATION W/ 'WANT TO HEAR ME YODEL?'

. . . .
. . . .
. . . .
. . . .
. . . .
. . . .
. . . .
. . . .
. . . .
. . . .
. . . .

———————— WHAT'S YOUR REVIEW? ————————

EXHIBIT A

GO SEE THE NORTHERN LIGHTS—AND MAYBE GRAB SOME POUTINE WHILE YOU'RE UP THERE.

. . . .

. . . .

. . . .

. . . .

. . . .

. . . .

—————— WHAT'S YOUR REVIEW? ——————

FAST FOR THE WHOLE DAY. BUT WHAT YOU DECIDE TO DO REALLY FAST IS COMPLETELY UP TO YOU.

. . . .

. . . .

. . . .

. . . .

. . . .

. . . .

—————— WHAT'S YOUR REVIEW? ——————

HAVE A CONTINENTAL BREAKFAST
ON ALL SEVEN CONTINENTS.

. . . .

. . . .

. . . .

. . . .

. . . .

. . . .

———————— WHAT'S YOUR REVIEW? ————————

PLACE A CRAIGSLIST AD OFFERING YOUR
SERVICES AS A PROFESSIONAL 'WAKER-UPPER*'
AND SEE IF YOU GET ANY TAKERS.

*KNOWN AS A 'KNOCKER-UPPER' IN THE 1800s BUT, YEAH, DON'T SAY THAT.

. . . .

. . . .

. . . .

. . . .

. . . .

. . . .

———————— WHAT'S YOUR REVIEW? ————————

QUALIFY FOR THE OLYMPICS. SURE, GYMNASTICS IS GLAMOROUS AND ALL—BUT WE'D PROBABLY SHOOT FOR CURLING.

WHAT'S YOUR REVIEW?

EXHIBIT A

WHEN SOMEONE THAT YOU DON'T KNOW ASKS WHAT YOU DO FOR A LIVING, PRETEND TO BE SOMETHING ELSE—LIKE A MIME.

WHAT'S YOUR REVIEW?

EXHIBIT A

RENT OUT AN ENTIRE ROLLER RINK, SO YOU HAVE THE WHOLE THING TO YOURSELF—OKAY, MAYBE BRING A FRIEND FOR COUPLES SKATE.

. . . .
. . . .
. . . .
. . . .
. . . .
. . . .

WHAT'S YOUR REVIEW?

HAVE SEX ON AN EMPTY BEACH—WHILE DRINKING A 'SEX ON THE BEACH.' NOW FIGURE OUT WHICH WAS THE BIGGER LET DOWN.

. . . .
. . . .
. . . .
. . . .
. . . .
. . . .

WHAT'S YOUR REVIEW?

TALK YOUR WAY INTO, OR OUT OF, JURY DUTY—DEPENDING ON YOUR PERSONAL GOAL IN THE MATTER.

. . . .
. . . .

WHAT'S YOUR REVIEW?

FIND A BUILDING THAT IS SET TO BE DEMOLISHED AND ASK NICELY IF THEY'LL LET YOU HIT THE DETONATION BUTTON.

. . . .
. . . .

WHAT'S YOUR REVIEW?

ADOPT A DOG FROM THE SHELTER THAT YOU'LL LOVE MORE THAN ANYTHING—DESPITE IT DESTROYING EVERYTHING IN YOUR HOME.

. . . .
. . . .

WHAT'S YOUR REVIEW?

EAT SOME SEAFOOD THAT IS STILL ALIVE.
LIKE, BY DESIGN. DON'T JUST GET IMPATIENT
ABOUT THAT HALIBUT.

WHAT'S YOUR REVIEW?

DONATE YOUR HAIR TO LOCKS OF
LOVE. BONUS: GROW A PRETTY SWEET
MULLET IN THE PROCESS.

WHAT'S YOUR REVIEW?

GO FOR A RIDE IN A HOT AIR BALLOON—BECAUSE YOU HAVEN'T TRULY FLOWN UNTIL YOU'VE DONE IT IN A WICKER BASKET WITH NO STEERING.

WHAT'S YOUR REVIEW?

WHEN IT'S TIME TO MOVE ON FROM A JOB, HIRE A SKY WRITER TO SPELL OUT 'I QUIT' AND ASK YOUR BOSS TO LOOK OUT THE WINDOW.

WHAT'S YOUR REVIEW?

DRAW A TERRIBLE TATTOO FOR YOUR FRIENDS.
NOW MAKE THEM ALL PROMISE THAT THEY'LL
GET IT PUT ON THEIR ARMS IF YOU DIE.

DON'T HAVE A CANVAS HANDY? USE THIS:

SIGN YOUR MASTERPIECE

GO ON A WEEK-LONG CRUISE—AND COVERTLY LIST ALL OF THE 60+ YEAR OLDS THAT YOU SUSPECT OF BEING SWINGERS.

PRO-TIP: LOOK FOR PINEAPPLES ON DOORS.

NO PAPER? WELL, YOU'RE IN LUCK.

EAT SOME FUGU FISH—WHICH IS A DELICACY, AND ALSO EXTREMELY FATAL IF PREPARED INCORRECTLY. SO MAYBE DO THIS ONE LAST.

. . . .

. . . .

. . . .

. . . .

. . . .

. . . .

——————— WHAT'S YOUR REVIEW? ———————

DANCE ON THE TOP OF A BAR. NOTE: THIS CAN ONLY END TWO WAYS—AS A LEGEND, OR IN JAIL. SO LEARN HOW TO READ A ROOM FIRST.

. . . .

. . . .

. . . .

. . . .

. . . .

. . . .

——————— WHAT'S YOUR REVIEW? ———————

**BUILD A PIECE OF FURNITURE FROM SCRATCH.
IF IT TURNS OUT GREAT, PUT IT IN YOUR HOUSE.
IF IT DOESN'T—IT'LL MAKE A GREAT GIFT.**

. . . .

. . . .

. . . .

. . . .

. . . .

. . . .

——————— WHAT'S YOUR REVIEW? ———————

**GO TO YELLOWSTONE & SEE THE MAJESTY OF
OLD FAITHFUL—AND TAKE A PHOTO THAT LOOKS
LIKE IT'S COMING OUT OF YOUR BUTT.**

. . . .

. . . .

. . . .

. . . .

. . . .

. . . .

——————— WHAT'S YOUR REVIEW? ———————

LEARN TO MOONWALK LIKE MICHEAL JACKSON—BECAUSE HONESTLY, BUZZ ALDRIN WAS JUST KIND OF HOPPING AROUND AND CRAP.

. . . .
. . . .

WHAT'S YOUR REVIEW?

WATCH A SOLAR ECLIPSE—BUT DON'T TAKE THAT AS LITERALLY AS OUR 45TH PRESIDENT.

. . . .
. . . .

WHAT'S YOUR REVIEW?

HAVE HIGH TEA IN LONDON—BUT IF YOUR BUDGET IS TIGHT, JUST MAKE SOME EARL GREY WHILE YOU'RE HIGH.

. . . .
. . . .

WHAT'S YOUR REVIEW?

PUT FIREPLACE ASHES IN SMALL VIALS & ASK
YOUR FAMILY TO GIVE THEM TO EVERYONE THAT
COMES TO YOUR POST-CREMATION SERVICE.

WHAT'S YOUR REVIEW?

EXHIBIT A

HELP PAINT A GIANT MURAL—MAYBE EVEN SKETCH OUT YOUR OWN IDEAS FOR AN ACTUAL ARTIST TO COMPLETELY IGNORE.

DON'T HAVE A CANVAS HANDY? USE THIS:

SIGN YOUR MASTERPIECE

GO TO LAS VEGAS AND BET TWENTY BUCKS
ON BLACK AT THE FIRST ROULETTE WHEEL YOU
SEE. BOOM—YOU JUST LOST 20 BUCKS.

WHAT'S YOUR REVIEW?

STAY UP ALL NIGHT LONG, JUST
LIKE YOU USED TO DO WHEN THAT STILL
SOUNDED EVEN REMOTELY FUN.

WHAT'S YOUR REVIEW?

JOIN A COMPETITIVE ROLLER DERBY TEAM—RIGHT AFTER YOU INCREASE YOUR HEALTH CARE COVERAGE. DENTAL TOO.

WHAT'S YOUR REVIEW?

EXHIBIT A

STREAK A FOOTBALL GAME. YOUR FAMILY'S TRADITIONAL THANKSGIVING DAY GAME STILL COUNTS IN OUR BOOK.

· ·

· ·

—————— WHAT'S YOUR REVIEW? ——————

VISIT THE COUNTRY THAT YOUR ANCESTORS CAME FROM. IF YOU DON'T ACTUALLY KNOW, JUST PICK SOMEWHERE REALLY COOL.

· ·

· ·

—————— WHAT'S YOUR REVIEW? ——————

BUILD A SHIP IN A BOTTLE. PRO-TIP: WITH A BIG ENOUGH BOTTLE & A SMALL ENOUGH SHIP, YOU CAN JUST TOSS THAT SUCKER IN THERE.

· ·

· ·

—————— WHAT'S YOUR REVIEW? ——————

GO ON A ROAD TRIP TO SOMEWHERE THAT YOU'VE NEVER BEEN BEFORE, BUT ONLY USE A TRADITIONAL MAP TO GET THERE.*

*YOU'RE IN OUR THOUGHTS AND PRAYERS.

WHAT'S YOUR REVIEW?

VISIT ALL FOUR SELF-PROCLAIMED 'WORLD'S LARGEST' BALLS OF TWINE. BRING A TAPE MEASURE – LET'S SETTLE THIS.

WHAT'S YOUR REVIEW?

CALL YOUR PARENTS ON A WHIM, JUST TO TELL THEM THAT YOU LOVE THEM. THEY'LL PROBABLY THINK YOU'RE DRUNK, BUT IT'S OK.

WHAT'S YOUR REVIEW?

ENTER AN ICE CREAM EATING CONTEST—BUT ONLY AFTER MONTHS OF EXTENSIVE TRAINING. YOU DON'T WANT TO PULL ANYTHING.

WHAT'S YOUR REVIEW?

BUY A METAL DETECTOR & SPEND THE DAY LOOKING FOR TREASURE AT THE BEACH. DRAW WHAT YOU FOUND—AKA: BOTTLE CAPS.

DON'T HAVE A CANVAS HANDY? USE THIS:

SIGN YOUR MASTERPIECE

SPEND THE NIGHT IN AN ICE HOTEL—WHILE TRYING NOT TO THINK ABOUT HOW DUMB IT IS THAT YOU'RE ACTUALLY PAYING TO DO THIS.

WHAT'S YOUR REVIEW?

EXHIBIT A

WRITE A NOTE & HAVE IT SENT BY CARRIER PIGEON TO YOUR BEST FRIEND. WISH THEM HAPPY BIRTHDAY—IF IT'S LATE, BLAME THE PIGEON.

FLYPIGEON.CO — THIS ISN'T AN AD, WE JUST REALLY WANT PEOPLE TO DO IT.

——— NO PAPER? WELL, YOU'RE IN LUCK. ———

TRY SOME ROCKY MOUNTAIN OYSTERS.
DON'T ASK ANY QUESTIONS THOUGH, YOU'LL
RUIN THE FUN SURPRISE.

. . . .
. . . .

WHAT'S YOUR REVIEW?

LET A GIANT SNAKE COIL AROUND YOU.
LIKE, ONE THAT IS WITH A ZOO KEEPER OR
SOMETHING—NOT JUST OUT IN YOUR YARD.

. . . .
. . . .

WHAT'S YOUR REVIEW?

GO CROWD SURFING AT A CONCERT. ROCK
SHOWS ARE TOO EASY THOUGH. CHALLENGE
YOURSELF—TRY BLUEGRASS.

. . . .
. . . .

WHAT'S YOUR REVIEW?

BUY, AND LEARN HOW TO PLAY, A MINIATURE
VIOLIN — AND PULL IT OUT WHENEVER FRIENDS
START COMPLAINING ABOUT SOMETHING.

WHAT'S YOUR REVIEW?

EXHIBIT A

MAKE ONE OF THE LONDON PALACE GUARDS LAUGH — AND THEN HELP THEM FIND A REPLACEMENT JOB.

. . . .
. . . .
. . . .
. . . .
. . . .
. . . .
. . . .
. . . .
. . . .
. . . .

—————— WHAT'S YOUR REVIEW? ——————

EXHIBIT A

GO TO MARDI GRAS—BUT LET THE GIRLS
THERE KNOW THAT THOSE BEADS ARE LIKE
SUPER CHEAP ON AMAZON, SO RELAX.

- -

- -

- -

- -

- -

- -

WHAT'S YOUR REVIEW?

BUNGEE JUMP OFF OF A BRIDGE, BUT
NOT JUST BECAUSE ALL YOUR FRIENDS
ARE DOING IT.

- -

- -

- -

- -

- -

- -

WHAT'S YOUR REVIEW?

GET YELLED AT BY GORDAN RAMSEY. HONESTLY THOUGH, THIS SHOULD BE PRETTY EASY ONCE YOU FIND HIM.

. . . .

. . . .

. . . .

. . . .

. . . .

. . . .

WHAT'S YOUR REVIEW?

WALK THE ENTIRE LENGTH OF THE GREAT WALL OF CHINA—AS LONG AS YOU HAVE 422 VACATION DAYS TO SPARE.

. . . .

. . . .

. . . .

. . . .

. . . .

. . . .

WHAT'S YOUR REVIEW?

GO OUT & PROTEST FOR CAUSES THAT MAKE
A DIFFERENCE. BLACK LIVES MATTER. LGBTQIA+
RIGHTS. DAYLIGHT SAVING TIME IS STUPID.

SKETCH OUT SOME POTENTIAL PROTEST SIGNS:

SIGN YOUR MASTERPIECE

MAKE A LIST OF POTENTIAL VANITY LICENSE PLATE IDEAS FOR YOURSELF AND LET YOUR FRIENDS PICK THE WINNER.

POP EVERY BUBBLE IN A JUMBO ROLL OF
BUBBLE WRAP. ALSO, ANNOY EVERY PERSON
IN A 500 FOOT RADIUS.

. . . .
. . . .

——————— WHAT'S YOUR REVIEW? ———————

GO TO EVEREST, KANSAS, & CLIMB A MOUND.
NOW TELL EVERYONE THAT YOU CLIMBED MOUND
EVEREST WHILE KIND OF MUMBLING.

. . . .
. . . .

——————— WHAT'S YOUR REVIEW? ———————

SPRAY PAINT SOME GRAFFITI ON A WALL.
DO IT AT YOUR OWN PLACE THOUGH, UNLESS
YOU'RE A GIANT ASSHOLE.

. . . .
. . . .

——————— WHAT'S YOUR REVIEW? ———————

**LEARN TO WALK ON STILTS. I MEAN,
JUST THINK OF ALL THE MONEY THAT YOU'LL
SAVE ON LADDERS ALONE.**

. . . .

. . . .

. . . .

. . . .

. . . .

. . . .

——————— WHAT'S YOUR REVIEW? ———————

**GROW A HANDLE BAR MUSTACHE.
ADMITTEDLY, THIS COULD BE HARDER FOR
SOME MORE THAN OTHERS.**

. . . .

. . . .

. . . .

. . . .

. . . .

. . . .

——————— WHAT'S YOUR REVIEW? ———————

GO SWIMMING WITH THE DOLPHINS—EITHER THE UNDERWATER MAMMALS OR THE FOOTBALL TEAM. BOTH WOULD BE PRETTY GREAT.

— WHAT'S YOUR REVIEW? —

EXHIBIT A

CLIMB TO THE HIGHEST POINT IN THE STATE THAT YOU LIVE IN. RESIDE IN KANSAS? YOU'RE ALREADY THERE.

———————————— WHAT'S YOUR REVIEW? ————————————

EXHIBIT A

HUG AN OTTER. SURE, THAT'S NOT EVEN REMOTELY FUNNY—BUT IT WOULD BE THE BEST DAY EVER.

. . . .

. . . .

. . . .

. . . .

. . . .

. . . .

——————— WHAT'S YOUR REVIEW? ———————

MAKE A REAL SEX TAPE. WE'RE TALKING VHS, SO GOOD LUCK FINDING A CAMCORDER THAT WORKS.

. . . .

. . . .

. . . .

. . . .

. . . .

. . . .

——————— WHAT'S YOUR REVIEW? ———————

KEEP A SINGLE INDOOR PLANT LIVING FOR LONGER THAN TWO MONTHS.

WHAT'S YOUR REVIEW?

ROB A BANK. PRO-TIP: JUST LOOK FOR THAT LITTLE PLUG ON THE BOTTOM. YOUR KIDS WON'T EVEN KNOW THAT QUARTER'S MISSING.

WHAT'S YOUR REVIEW?

GO TO SUBWAY AND ASK THE SANDWICH ARTIST
TO MAKE YOU A FOOT LONG—BUT INSIST THAT
THEY ALSO DRAW A STILL LIFE OF IT.

DON'T HAVE A CANVAS HANDY? USE THIS:

SIGN YOUR MASTERPIECE

WRITE A FAN LETTER TO YOUR FAVORITE LIVING
MUSICIAN. WELL, YOU CAN PICK A DEAD ONE IF
YOU WANT, JUST DON'T EXPECT A RESPONSE.

**GO ON A WINERY TOUR AND SAMPLE ALL
OF THEIR WINES—AND FORGET THAT YOU EVER
TOURED A WINERY IN THE FIRST PLACE.**

. . . .

. . . .

. . . .

. . . .

. . . .

. . . .

———————— WHAT'S YOUR REVIEW? ————————

**GET YOUR CARICATURE DONE, BUT WHEN THEY
ASK WHAT YOUR HOBBIES ARE, SAY OSTRICH
FARMING—SO THEY HAVE TO DRAW YOU ON ONE.**

. . . .

. . . .

. . . .

. . . .

. . . .

. . . .

———————— WHAT'S YOUR REVIEW? ————————

LISTEN TO AM RADIO FOR AN ENTIRE DAY—OR JUST LET YOUR UNCLE RANT ABOUT NONSENSE & OCCASIONALLY WHISTLE. SAME THING.

. . . .

. . . .

. . . .

. . . .

. . . .

. . . .

———— WHAT'S YOUR REVIEW? ————

TRACK DOWN YOUR HIGH SCHOOL BULLY & RECONCILE—BY GIVING THEM A GIFT CARD TO A BUSINESS THAT CLOSED LAST MONTH.

. . . .

. . . .

. . . .

. . . .

. . . .

. . . .

———— WHAT'S YOUR REVIEW? ————

THROW YOUR DOG A HUGE BIRTHDAY PARTY AND INVITE ALL THE NEIGHBORHOOD DOGS. BUY PARTY HATS, TREATS, & A LOT OF POOP BAGS.

· ·
· ·

——————— WHAT'S YOUR REVIEW? ———————

RENT A LIMO AND HAVE THE DRIVER TAKE YOU TO A DOLLAR STORE. NOW GO INSIDE AND ASK TO BUY ONE OF EVERYTHING.

· ·
· ·

——————— WHAT'S YOUR REVIEW? ———————

HAVE YOUR FORTUNE TOLD—BUT INTERRUPT WITH 'I KNEW YOU WERE GOING TO SAY THAT' EVERY TIME THEY TRY TO TALK.

· ·
· ·

——————— WHAT'S YOUR REVIEW? ———————

SIGN UP FOR A PUB CRAWL, BUT GET VISIBLY
ANGRY AT EVERYONE ELSE THAT IS 'CHEATING'
BY WALKING—WHILE STAYING ON ALL FOURS.

WHAT'S YOUR REVIEW?

EXHIBIT A

DRAW A PICTURE OF YOUR DREAM DOG OR CAT & THEN GO AROUND TO EVERY SHELTER UNTIL YOU FIND ONE THAT MATCHES IT.

DON'T HAVE A CANVAS HANDY? USE THIS:

SIGN YOUR MASTERPIECE

BUY SOME TAP SHOES & TIPPTY-TAP-TAP-TAP
YOUR WAY THROUGH A LOCAL MALL—JUST LIKE
FRED ASTAIRE GOING TO A PANDA EXPRESS.

WHAT'S YOUR REVIEW?

WATCH THE RUNNING OF THE BULLS IN
SPAIN—OR THE LESSER-ATTENDED LAYING-DOWN
OF THE BULLS AT ANY LOCAL FARM.

WHAT'S YOUR REVIEW?

GO TO AN ITALIAN RESTAURANT W/ A DATE & ORDER SPAGHETTI ON 1 PLATE – BECAUSE YOU'LL BE EATING IT 'LADY & THE TRAMP' STYLE.

—————————— WHAT'S YOUR REVIEW? ——————————

EXHIBIT A

DRESS UP IN A SERIES OF VARIOUS DISGUISES TO GET FREE SAMPLES AT COSTCO—EVEN AFTER BEING TOLD THAT YOU DON'T NEED TO DO THAT.

WHAT'S YOUR REVIEW?

RIDE A MOTORCYCLE—OR EVEN BETTER, TALK YOUR FRIEND W/ A MOTORCYCLE INTO GETTING A SIDE CAR.

WHAT'S YOUR REVIEW?

TAKE THE PUBLIC BUS AND TRY TO GET A ROUND OF 'THE WHEELS ON THE BUS GO ROUND AND ROUND' STARTED.

WHAT'S YOUR REVIEW?

ENTER A CONTEST WHERE KEEPING YOUR HAND
ON A CAR THE LONGEST WINS—HOW DARE THEY
UNDERESTIMATE YOUR ABILITY TO NOT MOVE.

WHAT'S YOUR REVIEW?

GO PANNING FOR GOLD—BUT AFTER ABOUT
TWO HOURS OF LOOKING AT WET ROCKS, FEEL
FREE TO ASK WHEN IT'LL START BEING 'FUN.'

WHAT'S YOUR REVIEW?

SLIP A CAROUSEL OPERATOR $50 AND FINALLY SEE HOW MANY TIMES YOU CAN RIDE A MERRY-GO-ROUND IN A ROW BEFORE PUKING.

· ·

· ·

· ·

· ·

· ·

· ·

WHAT'S YOUR REVIEW?

GO INTO OUTER SPACE. SO FIRST, YOU'LL NEED TO BECOME FRIENDS WITH ELON MUSK. ACTUALLY NEVER MIND, IT'S NOT WORTH IT.

· ·

· ·

· ·

· ·

· ·

· ·

WHAT'S YOUR REVIEW?

DRAW UP SOME BLUEPRINTS FOR THE PERFECT TREE HOUSE — NEVER MIND THE KIDS, THIS ONE IS FOR YOU. INCLUDE A WET BAR.

DON'T HAVE A CANVAS HANDY? USE THIS:

SIGN YOUR MASTERPIECE

BUY A REALLY THICK ROPE, TAKE IT TO A BUSY SIDEWALK, AND START A GIANT GAME OF TUG OF WAR W/ THE PEOPLE WALKING BY.

WHAT'S YOUR REVIEW?

EXHIBIT A

**WRITE YOUR OWN SCANDALOUS MEMOIR,
THAT'S ONLY TO BE READ UPON YOUR DEATH.
IT'S TIME TO SPILL THE GOOD STUFF.**

. . . .
. . . .
. . . .
. . . .
. . . .
. . . .
. . . .
. . . .
. . . .
. . . .
. . . .
. . . .
. . . .
. . . .
. . . .
. . . .
. . . .
. . . .
. . . .

DRESS UP LIKE A PRIEST & HIDE IN A PUBLIC PLACE—NOW EVERY TIME SOMEONE SNEEZES, JUST JUMP OUT AND YELL 'BLESS YOU!'

. . . .
. . . .

WHAT'S YOUR REVIEW?

MAKE AS MUCH JELL-O AS HUMANLY POSSIBLE & HAVE A GIANT FOOD FIGHT—OUTSIDE. UNLESS YOU ARE FINE WITH BEING MURDERED.

. . . .
. . . .

WHAT'S YOUR REVIEW?

INVEST $100 IN CRYPTOCURRENCY—INSURING THAT YOU'LL EITHER BE A BILLIONAIRE, OR, MORE LIKELY, $100 POORER.

. . . .
. . . .

WHAT'S YOUR REVIEW?

HIRE A PRIVATE EYE TO INVESTIGATE YOURSELF
& SEE WHAT KIND OF DIRT THEY DIG UP. BONUS
IF IT'S STUFF YOU DIDN'T EVEN KNOW YOU DID.

--- WHAT'S YOUR REVIEW? ---

EXHIBIT A

FLY IN A PLANE, RIDE ON A TRAIN, AND TAKE
A CAR—ALL IN ONE DAY. NOW YOU KNOW WHAT
A DAILY COMMUTE IS LIKE INTO NYC.

· ·

· ·

· ·

· ·

· ·

· ·

· ·

· ·

· ·

· ·

—————— WHAT'S YOUR REVIEW? ——————

EXHIBIT A

TEACH THE CITY RATS TO BRING YOU DROPPED MONEY IN RETURN FOR BITS OF CHEESE.

. . . .

. . . .

. . . .

. . . .

. . . .

. . . .

——————— WHAT'S YOUR REVIEW? ———————

TAKE ADVANTAGE OF ALL OF THE LOCAL BIKE TRAILS IN YOUR AREA—BUT USE A POGO STICK INSTEAD.

. . . .

. . . .

. . . .

. . . .

. . . .

. . . .

——————— WHAT'S YOUR REVIEW? ———————

GO TO A SOUVENIR SHOP AND REFUSE TO LEAVE UNTIL THEY GIVE YOU A KEY CHAIN W/ YOUR ACTUAL NAME SPELLED CORRECTLY.*

*OUR HEARTS GO OUT TO THE SAOIRSE RONANS OF THE WORLD.

- -

- -

- -

- -

- -

- -

————————— WHAT'S YOUR REVIEW? —————————

LEARN TO DRIVE A SEMI TRUCK, JUST TO SAY YOU CAN—BUT ALSO SO YOU CAN WEAR TRUCKER HATS WITHOUT FEELING LIKE SUCH A FRAUD.

- -

- -

- -

- -

- -

- -

————————— WHAT'S YOUR REVIEW? —————————

PAINT ALONG TO AN OLD EPISODE OF 'THE JOY OF PAINTING' AND QUICKLY REALIZE THAT YOU ARE IN OVER YOUR HEAD.

DON'T HAVE A CANVAS HANDY? USE THIS:

SIGN YOUR MASTERPIECE

WRITE A LETTER TO SANTA & MAIL IT TO YOUR PARENTS—JUST TO MAKE SURE THEY KNOW THAT YOU FIGURED IT OUT. EVENTUALLY.

START LISTENING TO 'TOAD THE WET
SPROCKET' AGAIN—ONLY BECAUSE I'M SURE
THOSE GUYS WOULD APPRECIATE IT.

. . . .
. . . .

——— WHAT'S YOUR REVIEW? ———

EAT FOOD FROM A STREET VENDOR
IN EVERY COUNTRY THAT YOU EVER VISIT—JUST
CHOSE WISELY (& PACK PEPTO-BISMOL).

. . . .
. . . .

——— WHAT'S YOUR REVIEW? ———

SETTLE ALL FUTURE DISAGREEMENTS ONLY W/
ARM WRESTLING—SORRY GRANDMA, LOOKS LIKE
IT IS IN FACT YOUR TURN TO DO THE DISHES.

. . . .
. . . .

——— WHAT'S YOUR REVIEW? ———

TRY TO BECOME ONE WITH NATURE, UNTIL REALIZING THAT MEANS SLEEPING OUTSIDE—AND THAT'S WHERE BEARS TEND TO BE.

. . . .

. . . .

. . . .

. . . .

. . . .

. . . .

. . . .

. . . .

. . . .

. . . .

——————— WHAT'S YOUR REVIEW? ———————

EXHIBIT A

SELL SEA SHELLS BY THE SEA SHORE, AND FINALLY PUT THAT SALLY OUT OF BUSINESS ONCE AND FOR ALL.

— WHAT'S YOUR REVIEW? —

ACTUALLY FIND SOME DAMN QUICKSAND. SERIOUSLY, WHY WERE WE LED TO BELIEVE THAT THIS STUFF WAS EVERYWHERE?

— WHAT'S YOUR REVIEW? —

LEARN HOW TO SNOW SKI—FOLLOWED QUICKLY BY GETTING WAY TOO CONFIDENT AND ROLLING DOWN A HUNDRED FOOT HILL.

. . . .

. . . .

. . . .

. . . .

. . . .

. . . .

———— WHAT'S YOUR REVIEW? ————

STEAL CANDY FROM A BABY—BUT THEN FEEL REALLY GUILTY ABOUT IT AFTERWARDS, CAUSING YOU TO REFLECT ON ALL THE LIFE CHOICES THAT YOU'VE MADE TO GET TO THIS POINT IN YOUR LIFE WHERE YOU'RE STEALING CANDY FROM AN ACTUAL BABY.

. . . .

. . . .

. . . .

. . . .

———— WHAT'S YOUR REVIEW? ————

THINK YOU CAN DO BETTER? LET'S SEE IT. NOW IT'S YOUR TURN TO COME UP WITH YOUR OWN 'MUST-DOS'...AND, WELL, DO THEM.

DON'T STOP WITH ONE. USE THE NEXT FEW PAGES TOO.

NO PAPER? WELL, YOU'RE IN LUCK.

THINGS TO DO BEFORE YOU DIE • NOW IT'S YOUR TURN

_____

_____

. . . .

. . . .

. . . .

. . . .

. . . .

. . . .

———————————— **WHAT'S YOUR REVIEW?** ————————————

THINGS TO DO BEFORE YOU DIE • NOW IT'S YOUR TURN

_____

_____

. . . .

. . . .

. . . .

. . . .

. . . .

. . . .

———————————— **WHAT'S YOUR REVIEW?** ————————————

WHAT'S YOUR REVIEW?

WHAT'S YOUR REVIEW?

THINGS TO DO BEFORE YOU DIE · NOW IT'S YOUR TURN

WHAT'S YOUR REVIEW?

THINGS TO DO BEFORE YOU DIE · NOW IT'S YOUR TURN

WHAT'S YOUR REVIEW?

THINGS TO DO BEFORE YOU DIE · NOW IT'S YOUR TURN

_____

_____

. . . .

. . . .

. . . .

. . . .

. . . .

. . . .

————————— WHAT'S YOUR REVIEW? —————————

THINGS TO DO BEFORE YOU DIE · NOW IT'S YOUR TURN

_____

_____

. . . .

. . . .

. . . .

. . . .

. . . .

. . . .

————————— WHAT'S YOUR REVIEW? —————————

THINGS TO DO BEFORE YOU DIE · NOW IT'S YOUR TURN

WHAT'S YOUR REVIEW?

THINGS TO DO BEFORE YOU DIE · NOW IT'S YOUR TURN

WHAT'S YOUR REVIEW?

THINGS TO DO BEFORE YOU DIE · NOW IT'S YOUR TURN

WHAT'S YOUR REVIEW?

THINGS TO DO BEFORE YOU DIE · NOW IT'S YOUR TURN

WHAT'S YOUR REVIEW?

THINGS TO DO BEFORE YOU DIE • NOW IT'S YOUR TURN

WHAT'S YOUR REVIEW?

THINGS TO DO BEFORE YOU DIE • NOW IT'S YOUR TURN

WHAT'S YOUR REVIEW?

NOW WRITE DOWN SOME THINGS THAT YOU'VE ALREADY DONE THAT FEEL LIKE BUCKET LIST ACCOMPLISHMENTS—FOR POSTERITY.

PSST: SHARE THEM WITH US @BRASSMONKEYGOODS

· ·

· ·

· ·

· ·

· ·

· ·

· ·

· ·

· ·

· ·

· ·

· ·

· ·

· ·

· ·

· ·

· ·

· ·

· ·

NO PAPER? WELL, YOU'RE IN LUCK.

THINGS YOU'VE ALREADY DONE BEFORE YOU DIE

WHAT'S YOUR REVIEW?

THINGS YOU'VE ALREADY DONE BEFORE YOU DIE

WHAT'S YOUR REVIEW?

THINGS YOU'VE ALREADY DONE BEFORE YOU DIE

WHAT'S YOUR REVIEW?

THINGS YOU'VE ALREADY DONE BEFORE YOU DIE

WHAT'S YOUR REVIEW?

THINGS YOU'VE ALREADY DONE BEFORE YOU DIE

WHAT'S YOUR REVIEW?

THINGS YOU'VE ALREADY DONE BEFORE YOU DIE

WHAT'S YOUR REVIEW?

THINGS YOU'VE ALREADY DONE BEFORE YOU DIE

. . . .
. . . .
. . . .
. . . .
. . . .
. . . .

——————— **WHAT'S YOUR REVIEW?** ———————

THINGS YOU'VE ALREADY DONE BEFORE YOU DIE

. . . .
. . . .
. . . .
. . . .
. . . .
. . . .

——————— **WHAT'S YOUR REVIEW?** ———————

THINGS YOU'VE ALREADY DONE BEFORE YOU DIE

_____

_____

. . . .
. . . .
. . . .
. . . .
. . . .
. . . .

——————— **WHAT'S YOUR REVIEW?** ———————

THINGS YOU'VE ALREADY DONE BEFORE YOU DIE

_____

_____

. . . .
. . . .
. . . .
. . . .
. . . .
. . . .
. . . .

——————— **WHAT'S YOUR REVIEW?** ———————

THINGS YOU'VE ALREADY DONE BEFORE YOU DIE

WHAT'S YOUR REVIEW?

THINGS YOU'VE ALREADY DONE BEFORE YOU DIE

WHAT'S YOUR REVIEW?

BRASSMONKEYGOODS.COM

✖

@BRASSMONKEYGOODS 📷